Leisure Arts 41

Painting
Wild Animals in
Watercolour

Sally Michel

SEARCH PRESS

Introduction

Essentially, there is no difference between painting wild and domestic animals. It takes more trouble to observe wild ones, and the view will be more distant, but the same principles apply. Observation is the starting point, and may be supplemented by knowledge gained from photographs, studying skeletons and stuffed specimens in museums, and reading.

Most places have some wildlife, particularly birds such as sparrows, pigeons and gulls. However, this book deals only with mammals. One of these is outstandingly accessible; the maligned but lively and attractive grey squirrel is found in almost every city park, and in many gardens which even in towns may also be visited by foxes and hedgehogs.

A wish to paint wildlife often develops from an interest in watching animals. Likewise, starting to draw them without prior knowledge will stimulate an interest in their habits and way of life, in the slight differences between closely related varieties, the similarities between one species and another, and the whole fascinating subject of evolution.

Materials and equipment

You will need equipment for working at home, and for working at zoos, parks, and in the countryside. The first essentials are a small sketch-book and a pencil, so that any sight of a wild creature can be noted; even the slightest of drawings will help you to recall much about the subject.

Colours

The more expensive Artists' watercolours are worth buying, as they go further than cheaper ones and are easier to use. A few carefully chosen colours can be added to later. The pigments that I use most are burnt sienna, yellow ochre (or raw sienna), lamp black, Payne's grey, cadmium lemon or Winsor yellow, and phthalocyanine blue. You could manage reasonably well with these six, from which you could mix the whole range of browns from the palest cream to near black, yellowish and red-browns, all blacks and greys, and the greens and browns of natural backgrounds.

Other colours which will be useful, although used in far smaller quantities, may be added gradually, as need dictates. These might include cadmium scarlet, quinacridone pink (permanent rose), Winsor violet (useful for mixing rich subtle browns), French ultramarine or cobalt blue, and cadmium yellow or cadmium yellow light (not chrome yellow, which is unstable). This deeper yellow will increase the variety of greens that you can obtain.

I also use white, but I prefer gouache zinc white to watercolour, as I often want light detail on a darker background and gouache is far more dense than a watercolour white.

Brushes

Always buy the best brushes that you can afford. I suggest that you obtain a few very fine ones, Nos. 0 or 00, for individual hairs and whiskers. I like to have one or two very long-haired brushes (riggers) for this purpose. You will also need several medium-sized brushes, Nos. 4 to 7. If the longer ones are too expensive in pure sable, then there are excellent nylon and nylon/sable mixtures available. It is useful to have one really big brush, No. 10 or larger. This could be of nylon or one of the cheaper, softer hairs.

Pencils

I recommend 2H, H or F grade pencils for fine detail, and HB or B grade ones for quick sketches. Also useful is a lump of putty rubber.

Papers

You will need a large amount of cheap cartridge paper for sketching from life or television, for roughs, and for working out compositions for finished paintings. Good watercolour paper should be used for finished work, and I recommend a good quality mould-made rag paper or a handmade one if possible. The same painting on indifferent and on good quality paper will be unbelievably different, both in ease of execution and in the finished effect.

Drawing boards

I use the conventional solid half-imperial and, when needed, imperial drawing boards in the studio. For work in the field I use small boards of three-ply, with rounded corners, which are light in weight and can be carried conveniently in a portfolio.

Other equipment

A small simple camera is an invaluable piece of equipment, providing a supplementary record of the animal being drawn. I find these photographs very useful for supplying details of markings and colour, particularly if the creature that I am drawing moves before I have finished it.

Another essential part of a professional wildlife artist's equipment is a reference – a collection of photographs, including those you take yourself, of all the animals you want, or might ever in the future want or need, to paint. No newspaper or magazine is ever thrown away without being scanned for photographs, bookshops are rummaged through for books with useful shots of animals, and these are kept to refer to – never, it must be emphasized, to copy. The image in the photograph is the property of the photographer; you may use it to supply information, to supplement or confirm your own knowledge, but you may not reproduce it.

Stage 1

Stage 2

A resting tiger: demonstration

Original size: 280 × 290mm (11 × 11½in)
Paper: Bockingford, 425gsm (200lb)

There is no point in making unnecessary difficulties for yourself, so it is sensible to begin with an animal which is asleep or at rest. A large carnivore which has no need to hunt for its food, waiting more or less contentedly for the next meal to be delivered to its zoo enclosure, is a good subject. A lion or tiger is sufficiently like a domestic cat to be reasonably familiar in appearance, which is helpful, and either is likely to lie fairly still for a long time, giving you time to study and draw.

Stage 1

A careful drawing is made with an F grade pencil on a heavy weight Bockingford paper, paying particular attention to details such as toes and facial features.

Stage 2

The background consists of simple washes, using only two colours, to provide a contrast of colour without requiring a lot of work on the setting. The paper is wetted all over the sky area with clean water, a thin wash of cobalt blue and manganese blue applied, and the clouds blotted out with a piece of dampened kitchen paper. When it is dry, the bottom part is given a wash of blue-green mixed from phthalocyanine blue and cadmium yellow (light). Once this is half dry, extra colour is added around the feet and the lower edge of the tiger's body.

Stage 3

A mixture of yellow ochre, burnt sienna, and a little cadmium scarlet is washed over the tiger's coloured areas, softening the edges where needed. More colour is applied to the head and nose just before the wash dries.

Stage 4 – the finished painting

The stripes, pads, details of eyes, nose, ears, and toes are added using a black wash of varying strengths, with a

Stage 3

Stage 4 – the finished painting

thin wash of black on the nose and chest. White body-colour is used for the whiskers and for hairs on the tail, face, paws, and body.

Observing and drawing

Whatever medium is intended for carrying out a painting, it must start with drawing. After years of experience, an artist may base his picture on a sketch so apparently slight that it seems almost as if the drawing stage is being bypassed. For this to be done successfully, careful study and observation must have been carried out in the past, over many years, so that the artist's stored knowledge of the subject enables him to sum up very quickly the essential facts of the model before him, and to add these to what is already in his memory, to produce a true and completely understood presentation of what is there. Until this study has been done, it is as well to spend as much time as you can on drawing, and on the careful exploratory looking which is its necessary preliminary and accompaniment. Even if you have no immediate intention of doing a painting, no time spent on drawing is wasted; carry a sketch-book with you, and draw whenever possible. Practice in drawing, on any subject, increases your ability to draw any other subject, so that even if the result appears to be of little significance, it has a beneficial effect on your general ability. By filling sketch-books with drawings of many different animals you are building up your knowledge of their structure and habits, and also a useful record to refer to for later work. Do not be disheartened at the apparent impossibility of completing any one drawing – even the smallest sketch can be useful. Start another drawing if your subject moves, as you may well have a chance later to go back to the first one. Keep all your drawings, however incomplete, and make written notes about colours, behaviour, the age and sex of the animal, and anything else that contributes to your knowledge. Label and date all your drawings, not forgetting to include the year. Try to draw from different viewpoints, and pay attention to the structure of eyes, feet, and ears.

If you come across animals by the roadside which have been killed by traffic but not too badly damaged, then these can be invaluable, as through them you can discover the exact structure of feet, ears, fur growth patterns and other such details, and make measured drawings. Draw the head, or limbs, from different viewpoints, and use these studies in conjunction with your drawings from the living animal. They will help you to make a really well observed and thoroughly worked out painting. Some drawings of this kind are shown here, and some of this type of material has been used for the grey squirrel demonstration painting which follows.

Grey squirrel: demonstration

Original size: 290 × 222mm (11½ × 8¾in)
Paper: Mould-made Saunders, 300gsm (140lb)

Stage 1
Firstly, drawings of squirrels are made from life, and then one is chosen to be redrawn and enlarged, together with a background of tree trunk, branches and leaves to complete the composition.

Stage 2
A wash of pale reddish brown, composed of burnt sienna with a little yellow ochre, is put over those parts of the squirrel on which the longer grey fur does not completely obscure the brown. A paler, more yellow wash is added around the eye, and a pale pink is used for the inside of the ear. A wash of grey is then applied over the whole squirrel, except for the white chest, stomach and chin, the inside of the ear, and the area around the eye, allowing the colour to become very much thinned out over the reddest parts.

Stage 1

Stage 2

Stage 3

A very pale cobalt blue wash is put on the sky, yellow-green is applied to the trees in the background, and a deeper green is used on the leaves above the squirrel. These washes of green should not be flat, but should have variations of colour and tone. Yellowish, and bluer, deeper tones are used to give variety and form without going into much detail.

A dark brown wash is applied over the trunk and limbs of the tree, using a mixture of burnt sienna, black, and a little violet. When this wash is half dry, a very strong mixture of the same colour is used to define the texture of the bark and the edges of the leaves at the top. The squirrel's eye is added in black; just before it is dry, water is dropped into the middle and blotted up with a squeezed-out brush.

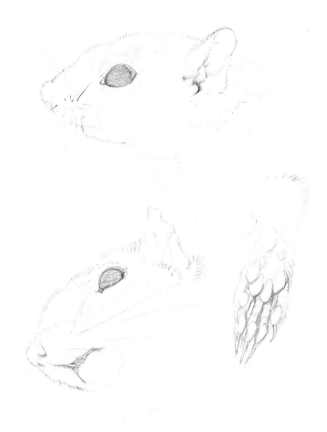

Stage 3

Stage 4 – the finished painting

Next, the ears, toes, claws, and nose are defined with a fine brush, and many hairs are added. Long hairs are applied to the tail; firstly, black and very dark grey ones over the central part, and then white ones, mainly around the edges with a few over the central part. These long white hairs form a diffuse outer zone all over the tail, but the reddish colour still shows through, as it does through the similar layer of black hairs which underlie the white. Short hairs are put in on the squirrel's body, head, and feet, and the whiskers finish the painting.

Stage 4 – the finished painting

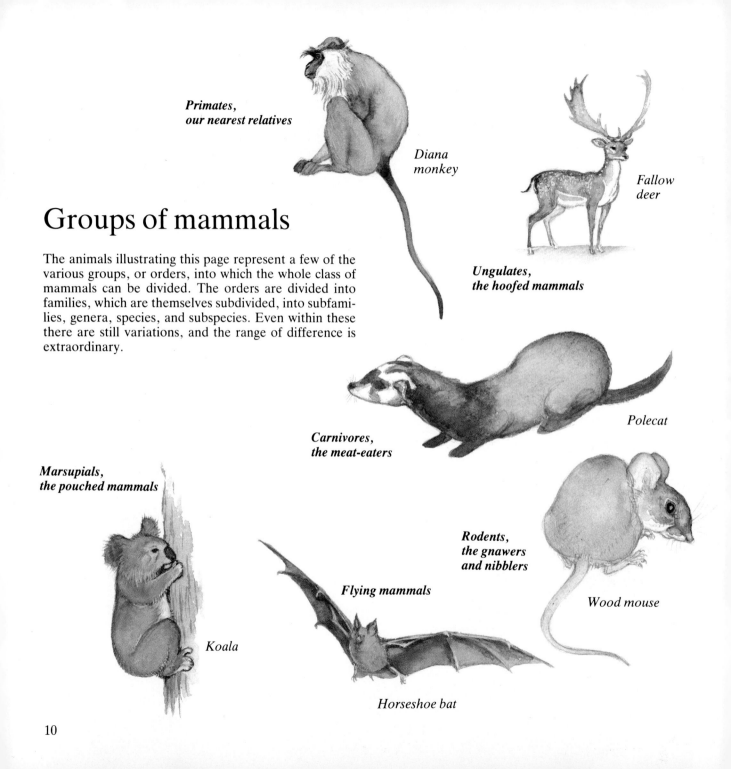

**Primates,
our nearest relatives**

Diana
monkey

Fallow
deer

**Ungulates,
the hoofed mammals**

Groups of mammals

The animals illustrating this page represent a few of the various groups, or orders, into which the whole class of mammals can be divided. The orders are divided into families, which are themselves subdivided, into subfamilies, genera, species, and subspecies. Even within these there are still variations, and the range of difference is extraordinary.

**Carnivores,
the meat-eaters**

Polecat

**Marsupials,
the pouched mammals**

**Rodents,
the gnawers
and nibblers**

Flying mammals

Wood mouse

Koala

Horseshoe bat

Fox: demonstration

Original size: 225 × 225mm (9 × 9in)
Paper: Mould-made Whatman, 180gsm (90lb)

The subject of this demonstration, the running fox, presents the problem of dealing with the moving animal. Familiarity with the animal's anatomy, through studying the skeletal structure, will help in analysing what underlies the movements of the running animal; the positions of legs, head, tail, and so on. The more that you draw the living animal, the easier it will become. Also, simply watching attentively for a time, without drawing, is useful, especially if the opportunity arises to watch the movement on a slow-motion film.

Stage 1
The figure of the fox is carefully drawn, using many studies from life and from filmed wild animals. Details and measurements are checked by reference to photographs and to measured drawings made from dead specimens. This is then developed into a pen drawing, with the essentials completed but the finishing to be done later.

Stage 1

Stage 2

Stage 3

Stage 2

Pale washes are applied: cobalt blue for the sky; blue-green for the field; and yellow ochre and a variety of greens for the foreground, some bright and yellowish, some with more blue.

Stage 3

This process is taken further, using a blue/grey/green for the bush on the right of the picture, yellow-olive for the oak trees in the background, and a brighter green for the other distant trees. A mixture of green, yellow, and brown is applied to the fence posts, burnt sienna to the sorrel, and yellow ochre to the dried stalks of the cow parsley. Dots of yellow are used for the flowers, dark green for the nettles, and a stronger, bluer green for the clumps of reeds. A basic wash of burnt sienna is then put over the figure of the fox.

Stage 4 – the finished painting

The figure of the fox is now completed with a black wash of varying strengths; intense on the feet and muzzle, and thin on the body and tail. The texture of the paper complements this combination of two separate washes.

A great deal of detail is added to the background, using watercolour for the bright yellow-green leaves around the left-hand fence post and foliage, and pen for the details of branches, leaves, grass, reeds, posts, and wire. The fox is treated in a similar way, with watercolour being used for the whitish hairs on the tail, head, neck, chest, and rump, and pen for the details of hairs, toes, claws, whiskers, and eye.

Stage 4 – the finished painting

Ungulates – the hoofed mammals

This is a large group, comprising much of what we eat – beef, mutton, pork and venison on the hoof, which are mainly domesticated in this country – and much that carnivores eat in other parts of the world – antelopes, gazelles, zebras, giraffes, and buffaloes. It also includes the wild cattle, sheep, pigs, goats, and horses from which our farm animals are derived.

In Britain, wild ungulates are not easily seen, although semi-wild deer and ponies can be spotted in parks and such places as the New Forest, Dartmoor, and the Scottish Highlands. These animals, despite being owned and managed, live much as wild ones would, and are not significantly different in form, although culling can affect their colour, as in the case of the 'black' fallow deer of Epping Forest. Wild species can be seen in zoos and zoo parks, and some of these have played a crucial part in preserving certain species. For example, Père David's deer, extinct in its native China, continued to exist at Woburn Park thanks to a former Duke of Bedford. Herds of deer have long adorned great estates and can be seen at close quarters – occasionally too close for the comfort of picnicking visitors. However, ungulates are not the easiest of animals to draw. Their anatomy is exposed and their bones much in evidence, so that there is little opportunity of burying imperfections of draughtsmanship in long hair. Young ungulates are often attractively marked; most deer have spotted calves, and the babies of European wild swine have longitudinal stripes.

Zoos and zoo parks

Whatever the ethical arguments against zoos, they provide a means of studying and drawing wild animals at closer quarters than is possible in the open. Boredom and familiarity with humans induce many animals to remain in sight for long enough to be drawn and closely observed – an irreplaceable benefit. I try not to carry too much equipment when I go to a zoo, but use memory, a camera, and previously collected reference material in combination with my drawings to produce finished coloured work in the studio. I prefer to use the time available to study form and movement, simply making notes of colours on the drawings. Looking at these later on revives my memory for colouration, although form was my principal preoccupation whilst drawing.

I carry a small portfolio, plenty of cheap paper for drawings, a small light drawing board, and ready-sharpened pencils of several grades. I find a B grade soft enough, and use a well-pointed F or H grade when great speed is not needed; the faster the work, the softer the

pencil used. Pencils must be kept sharpened, and a knife or some sandpaper is an essential tool. A jacket of the kind favoured by walkers is useful, as the many pockets allow me to carry pencils, erasers, camera, and everything else I need, without the weight becoming oppressive, and it leaves both my hands free.

I also take any paintings that I may be working on, so that if I have the opportunity I can check the drawing and improve their liveliness and authenticity by working, even very briefly, from the living animal. It is helpful to take photographs of what you have been drawing, and also to visit the zoo's shop and buy its postcards, which often portray the zoo's own specimens, possibly the ones that you have been drawing, in photographs of excellent quality.

The prevailing tendency in zoos seems to be for the number of species kept to be reduced, but, increasingly, for those species to be maintained in groups of a size that encourages successful breeding.

Using photography and television

It is difficult always to work directly from nature with wildlife subjects. If you work from zoo specimens, then the question of the background still remains, and it is often necessary to seek further information about the details of an animal's appearance. Although it is better to draw from life as far as possible, photographs, television, and video films can be used quite legitimately to supply the deficit, although they must never simply be copied but rather used as an extra source of information. I draw a great deal from television nature films. The drawings are rough and incomplete, but they have a liveliness that comes only from watching the movement

of an animal going about its normal business. These sketches provide the framework; the rest is supplied by memory, knowledge, photographs, studies done from closer quarters of zoo specimens, and sometimes from looking at dead or stuffed animals. Dead animals should be used with care, simply to gain information about their markings, hair patterns, and structural details. Otherwise, it is possible to portray the deadness of the animal too faithfully. Video recordings can be of great help, particularly to slow down movement enough for analysis and understanding. It is important not to work from a still image alone.

The painting above has been composed from various sources. Drawings of the individual animals done at zoos and from television have been used for the lioness, zebras, and elephants, whilst the generalized East African savannah background has been made up of elements from film and photographs of the kind of terrain where the species illustrated are found.

Primates –
our nearest relatives

This order includes, among many other species, the bush-babies, lemurs, marmosets, monkeys, and our close relatives the man-like apes, of which the chimpanzee is very close indeed.

The true lemurs are all native to the island of Madagascar and found nowhere else. The ruffed lemur on this page and the ring-tailed lemur shown opposite are typical. They are wonderfully agile, marvellous climbers, handsomely coloured and patterned, and have human-looking hands and feet, weird voices, and a permanent look of astonishment.

The little cotton-headed tamarin at the bottom of page 21 is closely related to the marmosets and the New World monkeys.

Ring-tailed lemur:
demonstration

Original size: 285 × 300mm (11½ × 12in)
Paper: Whatman, 180gsm (90lb)

Many drawings and studies, done in past years, have helped me to compose the picture of the ring-tailed lemur walking, but there is a degree of truth in drawing which can be attained only by referring again to the living creature.

Stage 1

The drawing, lightly carried out on Whatman watercolour paper, is taken to a zoo with a colony of lemurs and this stage of the work is finished from life. Several sheets of new drawings are also made, on which to base more paintings in the future.

Stage 2

The whole background is very thoroughly wetted, up to within 5mm (¼in) or so of the edges of the lemur. A wash of green is then added from the top to about

Stage 1

Stage 2

half-way down the animal's legs, using deep blue-green at the top, graduating to a pale yellow-green, and taking the colour right up to its edges.

This is repeated from the bottom upwards, using a yellow-brown wash and allowing it to merge with the yellow-green without swamping it. The washes are not kept flat, and extra strong colour is added here and there.

Stage 3

Mixtures of strong blue-green in differing tones on the wooded background, deeper yellow-green on the grassy area, and yellow-brown on the bare earth of the foreground define the details and the edges of the lemur. When this is dry, a wash of burnt sienna is applied to the lemur's head and back, and yellow to its eyes.

Stage 4 – the finished painting (overleaf)

Washes of grey, firstly a blue-grey one, and when that is dry a weak black-and-water one, are put over all the grey parts of the lemur. A stronger black wash is used to define the mask, then a stronger one still for the fingers, toes, eyes, and tail-rings.

Stage 4 – the finished painting

Animal painting as portraiture

The family resemblance of the anthropoid apes to man is obvious when you draw and paint a portrait such as the one of the orang-utan shown here. All the features of the human physiognomy are there, although the proportions are different.

The briefest study of any group of orang-utans, or of gorillas or chimpanzees, will reveal considerable disparity between the faces of individual animals. Apart from the differences between males and females, adults and immature members of the group, the face of each one is as distinct and recognizable as those in any comparable group of humans. The variations are of the same kind as can be seen in humans and as subtle; slight differences in the length of the nose, the height of the forehead, or the width between the eyes. In other words, they are the same slight distinctions between one face and another as those which make it possible for us to tell all humans apart and which we perceive without difficulty.

This principle applies to any animal. At first glance the differences may not be apparent, but the more thorough the scrutiny the more obvious they become.

Patterns, patches, stripes and spots

A beautiful and attractive feature of many animals is the striking pattern of markings and colours on their coats. This has led to the appalling abuse of many species by the human race, who have slaughtered animals in countless thousands for the adornment of their own less attractive persons. All the spotted and striped cats have been victims, and when the dramatically furred and coloured colobus monkeys had the misfortune to attract the attention of the fashion trade some years ago they were mercilessly exploited.

The origin of the markings is, by contrast, unequivocally practical. They camouflage the owner and protect it from its enemies, whilst hiding it, if it is carnivorous, from its prey until it is in a position to prevent escape of the prey. Surprisingly, the spectacular stripes of a zebra cause it virtually to disappear in an open plain, as the markings shimmer and break up the form at a distance. The dark spots of a serval, the white spots and streaks on many species of deer, and the brown blotches of a giraffe, serve to help their owners disappear amongst the shadows of the leaves and branches. The beauty of the patterns is a by-product of utility.

Serval: demonstration

Original size: 335 × 290mm (13½ × 11½in)
Paper: Whatman, 300gsm (140lb)

This painting is of a serval, a pretty, graceful, smallish cat which dwells in many parts of Africa, from the savannah to riverside scrub. It is based on a drawing from a television wildlife film of the serval pausing to listen and look for possible prey. The work was completed from reference material and from the many careful studies of servals that I have done in the past, as this is a subject with which I am quite familiar. When I went to a zoo to check the painting, I found that it required almost no more work, which shows how valuable it is to draw as much as possible from life and to get to know your animal thoroughly.

Stage 1
As always, a thorough and careful drawing of the animal is essential.

Stage 1

Stage 2

A pale wash of ultramarine is put over the sky. When this is dry, a wash of yellow ochre, a little cadmium yellow, and burnt sienna is applied over the entire area, from the horizon downwards. Extra, stronger colour is added as it dries.

Stage 3

When the face, ears, chest, and two right legs are very nearly dry, a No. 3 or 4 brush loaded with clean water is used to dilute the colour in those areas. Then, squeezed almost dry, it is used to pick up the weakened wash from those parts. By this means, almost every trace of colour is removed where required.

The colour is then strengthened and deepened, with a little burnt sienna on the head, back, and shoulders, and yellow ochre inside the ears. When this is dry, very thin washes of black are applied to the head, shoulders, and rump, with a rather stronger mixture used for the nose. The twiggy bushes are completed with grey, using a fine brush.

Stage 4 – the finished painting

Stronger black builds up the pattern of spots and stripes, and the details of eyes, ears, and tail-tip. A thinner wash is used for the pale spots on the chest and belly, whilst a black and burnt sienna wash on the intermediate rows on the body completes the markings.

The final addition is the green foliage, ranging from pale bluish to strong yellowish green – just enough to balance the composition and echo the pattern of the serval's coat.

Stage 2

Stage 3

Stage 4 – the finished painting

Anatomical adaptations

Just as patterns of colour have evolved through their effectiveness in protecting an animal, enabling it to reach maturity and reproduce itself, so have anatomical differences developed, permitting the exploitation of a food source otherwise not available to it. Both of these effects will be seen in the same species. For example, the serval is protected by its camouflage of stripes and spots, and its overall colour; its extremely long legs and narrow body, so practical in a habitat of long grass and tall reeds, enable it to leap up and catch flying birds or to pounce on small rodents from above. Kangaroos and wallabies have evolved long, strong tails and disproportionately large hind legs, and they progress at speed by great leaps over distances. Giraffes' long necks and legs permit them to eat leaves far above the reach of other leaf-eaters, whilst submerged hippopotamuses can breathe and see what is going on above the surface because of their specialized eyes and nostrils. Other animals have webbed feet, and beavers' tails are shaped like paddles, so that they can move swiftly and effortlessly under water.

The route to drawing and painting an animal well is through the careful study of its form, leading to the perception of its physical entity. Understanding the purpose of the distinctive characteristics of an animal's shape and colouration can only increase your comprehension of the whole being, enhancing your power to portray it with insight. It also helps you to provide an authentic background.

The wallaby and joey are painted almost entirely with a wet wash, using burnt sienna mixed with yellow ochre. A thin lamp black is washed over the wet ground where required. The brown on the toes of the hind feet, the eyes, the inside of the ears, the noses, and the whiskers are added after the wash is dry, but the fine details are kept to an absolute minimum, and the character of the paper is allowed to play a major part in the picture.

My giraffe is shown in the open. After the initial stage – the careful drawing – the whole animal is given a wash of pale fawn, made from a weak mixture of burnt sienna and a little yellow ochre. This is taken only part of the way down the body and head and across the legs, and the edges of the wash are softened, leaving white paper on the chest, belly, and inner side of the legs.

Once this basic layer is completely dry, the pattern of brown patches is added, using a strong mixture of burnt sienna and a little violet. As this is applied, patch by patch, the colour is varied with water, or a little black, or a touch of cadmium scarlet, or extra yellow ochre and a lot more water, according to the nuances of colour and lighting.

Washes of pale grey are used to define the modelling of the face and ears, whilst a thinned wash of black is applied to the mane and to the darker muzzle and nose. A stronger black is used on the horns, tail and mane, with a little burnt sienna on the lower part of the mane.

The grass is done with a mixture of terre verte and yellow ochre applied to wetted paper, with long brush strokes continuing to the dry area above.

Stage 1

Stage 2

Harp seal: demonstration

Original size: 325 × 280mm (13 × 11in)
Paper: Not surface colour-wash board

One of the earliest manifestations of widespread interest in conservation, and of distaste for wholesale slaughter of animals whose food, bodies, or territory people want for themselves, was the concern for the fate of young harp seals butchered on the Newfoundland ice. Fortunately for the seals, their young have large melting eyes, furry little bodies, and voices like those of young children. Large numbers of people found the idea of clubbing and skinning them in front of their mothers repugnant, so the campaign was successful, for a time at least.

The harp seal picture is extremely simple in terms of colour; it is painted virtually in only three colours – pale blue, dull yellow, and a little black.

Stage 1
The drawing is done with almost all the work on the animal's head, the rest of the body being kept in the simplest of modes. Care in drawing the head is crucial – tread carefully the narrow path of careful and objective study of an appealing theme, and avoid the pitfall of mawkish sentimentality which often bedevils such subjects.

Stage 2
Pale blue – a thin wash of ultramarine – is used for the chilly sky. With the addition of a little Payne's grey, successively deeper washes indicate the broken surface of snow-covered ice. Keeping the colour pale in the distance, and deeper in the foreground, gives the effect of recession in a featureless landscape.

Stage 3 – the finished painting
Pale creamy fur, depicted with a thin wash of yellow ochre cooled down with a small addition of black, supplements the pencil drawing of the seal pup. Medium-strong to intense black is used to build up the small dark areas of fur on the muzzle and around the eyes, and to define the details of nostrils, mouth, eyes, and whiskers.

Stage 3 – the finished painting

Conservation

Gorillas and otters, notoriously shy animals, are both victims of human actions, their numbers catastrophically reduced through destruction of forests for agriculture, drainage and pollution of waterways, and intrusion on their habitats. These pictures are closely based on swiftly made drawings of wild ones seen on television films in their natural habitats, more information being supplied by photographs. In each case, the painting is a version of the drawing. The reference material has been used not to change the drawing, but only to add to it and to supply details necessarily left out whilst recording the essence of form and posture during the animal's brief appearance on the television screen.

The close relationship between the mature male silverback gorilla and man is obvious, in attitude, anatomy, and arrangement of features, although the proportions are different.

The otter, based on drawings of wild ones around the sea-lochs and shores of the western highlands of Scotland, is a fairly free brush drawing with wash, although time and care has been spent on getting the substructure right.

The desire for conservation of animals and their habitats has spread from a few so-called cranks,

regarded at the time as mad but harmless, to an increasing number of indisputably sane people who perceive that the world is not infinite, that damaging one part of it will affect the rest, and that although man is a successful, adaptable, and clever species it may be that he has allowed short-term greed to jeopardize his long-term future, along with that of every other living being.

Space travel and television have been partly responsible for this advance, showing that the Earth is, in cosmic terms, a tiny world of delicately balanced climate and vegetation. Photographs from space show the Earth's atmosphere – the only thing that keeps us alive and breathing – as a frighteningly thin layer of protection from the radioactivity of the sun and the unimaginable chill and emptiness of space.

Television, often abused, has been an irreplaceable source of information and education, showing the planet and the life on it to people who would otherwise have known comparatively little about it. Moving visual images in full colour combined with informed comment have reached further than words alone or still photography ever could, and have probably done more than anything to foster the growth of interest, most fortunately among children, in the state of the planet and the prospects for all its inhabitants.

There is no surer way of encouraging such interest than by drawing and painting animals, because this cannot be done without looking long and searchingly at the subject. That is the first step in any relationship, and once a relationship is established between us and wildlife, the urge to protect it is set in train.

First published in Great Britain 1992
Search Press Limited,
Wellwood, North Farm Road,
Tunbridge Wells, Kent TN2 3DR

Text, drawings and paintings by Sally Michel

ISBN 0 85532 690 5

Publishers' note
There are references to sable hair and other animal hair brushes in this
book. It is the Publishers' custom to recommend synthetic materials as
substitutes for animal products wherever possible. There are now a
large number of brushes available made of artificial fibres and they are
just as satisfactory as those made of natural fibres.

Distributors to the art trade:

UK

Winsor & Newton,
Whitefriars Avenue, Wealdstone,
Harrow, Middlesex HA3 5RH

USA

ColArt Americas Inc.,
11 Constitution Avenue, P.O. Box 1396, Piscataway, NJ 08855–1396

Arthur Schwartz & Co.,
234 Meads Mountain Road, Woodstock, NY 12498

Canada

Anthes Universal Limited,
341 Heart Lake Road South, Brampton, Ontario L6W 3K8

Australia

Max A. Harrell,
P.O. Box 92, Burnley, Victoria 3121

Jasco Pty Limited,
937–941 Victoria Road, West Ryde, N.S.W. 2114

New Zealand

Caldwell Wholesale Limited,
Wellington and Auckland

South Africa

Ashley & Radmore (Pty) Limited,
P.O. Box 2794, Johannesburg 2000

Trade Winds Press (Pty) Limited,
P.O. Box 20194, Durban North 4016

Composition by Genesis Typesetting, Rochester, Kent

Printed in Spain by Elkar S. Coop.